Sown at the seams with wildflowers

Sown at the seams with wildflowers

A collection of poems

Laura Roberts

Published by Tablo

Published in 2021 by Tablo Publishing.

Publisher and wholesale enquiries: orders@tablo.io

20 21 22 23 LSC 10 9 8 7 6 5 4 3 2 1

Sown at the seams with wildflowers

Stirring mushroom tea with a paintbrush in one hand, pen in the other. She utters no apology. Delving deep into the blue waters of her pure truth, she bathes, swims, drowns at times. But she can't be lost, only ever found. Discovering her very own magic, learning to wield the weapon of her choice.

There need be no witness to her coming home. The sacred lands of her body belong to her alone. She falls in love with colour and contour, swallows her words to savour the power of them.

Concentrated, her will is fire.

She has become the love she needs, relinquishing all expectation of the other. Relationship is born from sacred solitude.

She claims s p a c i o u s n e s s as her own, suspended in the strangeness of surrender and devotion to the unseen.

I am never alone where the land meets the sea
Where I meet she
The creator
Weaver
Of my innermost longings
I sing songs of gladness
Over the space between us
Knowing what awaits is something
Worth taking the time to grow strong enough to hold.
How can I fear the darkness
When that is where you revealed yourself to me?

I revel and play by moonlight
Hours alight with your whispering beauty
I found all of you there
Where I let all of myself be seen.

Poetry is my language
How did I not see until now?
How else can such a feeling be translated?

The lilting rhythm of my song
Awakens at sunrise
To sing adulations of the morning sun.

Every moment
A miracle by choice.

The medicine for grief is surely new life.

Sleep beckons me to follow
But I dare not give up the chase.
Will you still be here when I wake?

Inspiration.

If happiness is mine to hold
Can I shape it?
Make it my own
Make it impermeable
And permanent
If I could be so bold
As to assume its true form
Is something I can depend upon
When the fire in my heart
Turns cold.

When it does
I want to trust
I have a stronghold
That I can stand on the foundations I built
Spinning stories out of my heart as though they were made out
of silk
And that I spoke them well enough
For their wisdom to sink
Deep into my bones.

The rose gold glow of the day turning in
The flames of the sun
Burning up the stories
I have made as my offering
I wait inside the empty place I have made in my own heart
I learn to breathe through my fear
Of being alone in the dark

And I write.

I used to call these the lonely hours
But how I long to be alone with you
Pen in hand, no voice to disturb
Only the endless wandering
Through a night of stars.

Plucking each,
One by one
From the sky, to the empty page.

The moon licks her lips
Light drips from her mouth,
Parted in a sigh from which
A silver stream is flowing
Cascading down
Her bare body
Translucent, glowing
Bathing in the night
A second sigh
That look in her eye
Knowing I cannot fight this.

She writhes in the night
Can't sleep
Stirring from the deep
A feeling I can't resist
To caress her tender flesh
Drink in her moonlit skin
Surrendering.

So I submerge my being in her bliss

A life of longing
Surely worth
This kiss.

I feel you now
Where I couldn't
Sense you in places
Once told I shouldn't
Hide behind beauty
Rub colour on the washed out skin
Of these bodies
Dancing with grace.

I see you now
Where I couldn't
Hold you in ways
I otherwise wouldn't
No remedy for this madness
It is magic they warned us not to summon

Remember the art
The earth

The wild, untameable love

of Woman.

Friends laugh and share more than commonalities
They walk with each other
Whispering tales of home.

Colour is a cartwheel
A dance on slender stems
Their dresses all in disarray
Happiness unhemmed

So delicate is beauty
All effort woven underneath
The seed of their intention
A wish upon the wind.

Through conscious choice
We are painting the backdrop
For our children's dreams.

Has the thought occurred to you of what you would do
If I chose a different way?

I do not let myself imagine it often
My fear is a powerful destroyer
And I have chosen to be a creator of life.

I lay in the sunrise hour
Both hands protect the place
Where you once dwelt.

Is it strange that I can cry for you
And the short life you were dealt
When it was by my hand that you were woven
And unravelled again too soon
I feel you, in the softest hours
And every passing of the moon.

I feel you with every act of defiance
Against sacrilege to the sacred womb
You are the reason that I stand and speak
Weaving from creation's loom
Spin with strands whose depth of feeling
Is the beauty that I serve you with
You came and something in me died
Yet it died, so I would live

I owe no explanation.

I will write until I'm empty
Cry until there's nothing left to do
But pick myself up off the floor and trust.

With every step I carry us both.
You are perfect.

There is space enough to grow between the cracks of what has been and what's to come.

We plant flowers
In the garden of one another's body
I weep, raining my remaining fears
On the seeds I have planted
Nourishment to feed the dreams
I could not have imagined without her.

I don't know which of the words will find their way from the rug on my bedroom floor, where I sit by candlelight, to the pages of a book we'll place on the shelf someday.

I shall look at it all in wonder.

At last
I am home in a body
Whose bounds are sown at the seams
With wonder and wildflowers.

What has been and gone
In what feels like a blink of an eye
Has been rich in its beauty
Like a seed planted in soil
And roots connected by communication through the heart
I have been brought to life
Strong enough to hold
The dreams I contained
Through love and friendship
I have blossomed.

What does a wild prayer sound like?
A howl, a cry
Written by the roots, sent up to the sky
An ache that feels ancient
Carried by the trees
I pause, no longer certain
And lay among the leaves
It's there I take my breath, an offering, and lay it at her feet
Empty, I surrender, but tonight it's not so sweet

The agony of all that's lost to a world that cannot bear
To part with its monopoly on a truth that must be shared
We do not own the land, it was stolen, then divided
Our god is not a man yet it is man who has decided
To split her body open and take all that can be sold
A tidy profit at the cost of every living soul
Deprived of the journey to remember there's a choice
To ignore the forest's song or to listen to its voice.

And so I journey down, as deep as I dare
Empty still of breath, I choose Earth instead of air
The embers smoulder, a rage I can't express
Constrained by sensibility but if it's skin I can undress
Strip down to my bones, as dense and solid as she
Let the roots envelop, no longer I but we
Only then I soften, allow space for all that must arise
My own shadows plead with me to look them in the eye
I resist and I suffer, adamant it won't be felt
My fear of the void now greater than the void itself
The dam I built around the grief, cracks, flows out to the sea
I thought that I would drown in it but all I feel now, is free
A gasp, as life returns, words catch in my throat
Heart beat strong.

I reach for my clothes strewn on the forest floor
My bed among the roots feels like home once more
I gather up my breath, inhale deep into my lungs
I have become my prayer, I hear the song that must be sung
To creation, who - after all - might be, the wonder we've been
craving
I plant a seed in honour of the days I deem worth saving
Can we forgive ourselves the price, such ignorance has paid
Lay all that has been built to rest and find a way to start again
The wild prayers have saved my soul by remembering the Earth
The one with whom I share my breath

Exhale.

I am rebirthed.

The path between
each of my dreams
is a constellation.

I am guided by the light of a thousand stars.

She inspires love
And it rains and storms for the week I spend
In between
Floating on the ocean of the unknown
Yet all the time knowing perfectly
What we have created.
I knew to appreciate these nights
The space in between
How I love and honour my body
Her wisdom, her beauty
Her wild nature
Alive, pulsing with both our hearts.

I made my way to you
Holding half a sea of dreams

I look at the shape we make
And I know I'm home.

I thought I stole a glance
But it was gifted
She wanted me to see her bare
So that I would fall in love.

I find her in the forest
The scent of pine cones and dew
We meet under canopies
Of stars and storm clouds.

I always wait for her
Never leaving until I have felt
Beauty stir my heart
Where her songs dwell.

What will my mother say
When she discovers my god
Is a woman.

What of the strange visions that come to me
When the world goes quiet and dark
I'm a solitary woman
Prefer to dance alone by candlelight
In the presence of love and beauty
I find in the folds of paperbacks
And pockets of eternity.

There's less and less desire
To add my voice to the deafening chorus
But to listen to the sound of stillness that sings
It hums beneath it all.

I am comfortable here
In the body I have come to love
Familiar and intimate
I look at the world
Both belonging and not belonging
In the ways that seem to matter.

Lights go out
And I'm quieter than I've ever been
No inclination to explain myself
My choices
My precious peace

My tender love
Nurtured in the hours I share with God.

Who is God?

God is the part of me that found the courage to turn off the world
Distill my fear into art, silence and poetry.

My dreams are made more vivid
Rich with wonder having come from the place I have sought
And found
I trust these visions
Above and beyond the mirage of order and chaos.

I do not know how long I shall dwell here
But the door is closed
The clock has been put away.

I have no place else to be.

I pray a seed is planted
Inside every fertile mind
For nobody to fear
Letting the flowers in their heart bloom.

Nothing is actual
Not here, with the lights turned down
Mattress on the floor
I rest, days winding
Pages turning
My breath, hard to hear
When I'm not breathing.

I imagine so
And so it is
I find myself wearing my dreams on the outside
With every step I'm still surprised
That the ground has not given way to some kind of hell beneath
I have learned to be a little bit in love with everything
And move like somebody
Who belongs here
In this bliss.

Thoughts are dissonant
And stand at the entrance
To a land that is rightfully mine.

Whilst my mind is occupied
She waits, patiently
She needs attention, adoration
All I've been able to give her lately
Feel for myself how soft my skin is to the touch
Instead of waiting for someone for whom I'll always be too much or not enough.
I rub my own thighs, breasts and belly
Tell myself I'm home
And how much I've missed her.

Weigh me down, though she does
It's a kind Earth she ties me to
This mirror reflecting each thought in form
Tonight I feel infinite
At home in this temple, to which I've been born
The holy, wild feminine in form.

In our secret conversations
I pray
Let words find their way

From the stars to the page
Stepping stones
Across a river
Of unknown possibilities

Forgotten memories
Lost constellations

I am guided by a hand
Who has remembered
How to write

Her own destiny.

That line we draw between right and wrong
Blown away by the breath of stories
Told by our friends and strangers
Shouldn't that tell us something of its nature?
Fragile and unfitting for boundless hearts.

My ache
The crater left by your impact
Now fills when it rains
A wellspring of endless love
I learned to feel in your absence.
How can I dress you?
Hem you in with words
Pluck sentences from the sky of my mind
The threads of thought, woven by prayer
Into poetry to tell of how I found colour in the leaves
How I found the scent of jasmine
Or how it found me
And why the morning sun is my endless miracle.

I walk to your house on the hill
Pockets filled with herbs and sacred tobacco
We watch the changing colours of the sky
Trying to figure out what we want from love
Idly stroke each other's skin
Because it seems like the right way to say

I'm here for you.

He came in dressed in my dreams
Ones I keep between the seams
In pockets of silent power
I rarely let myself believe
I contain all I can conceive
Until he looked into my eyes
Cast a spell by spinning lies
To outshine the brightest star in my sky.

Disguised as a character I'd long forgotten
And forgotten, at last, to long for
What tide brought him, breathless to my shore
What door am I now to open
Hearing such words softly spoken
Awoken in my womb, a memory
A loom on which to thread
The fraying edge of a seamless vision
A prism of chaos into prayer.

I dare to see each movement
Interpret every meaning
I rewind in my mind to replay that perfect evening
We played our parts so effortlessly
We put aside the script
It was improvised
Now I wish

To dance a little longer
Upon that precipice
Where he had no beginning
And I no end.

Now pretend we did not mention
Or wonder at our own invention

Charmed, enraptured
With what intention did he fracture
The delicate shape of me?
I imagined him, at first
To weave that mirage into verse
To become what I saw you witness
Now what beauty I adorn you with
Is mine to do with what I wish
I used to want to play the muse
Until I became the artist.

Fools are made of lovers who have not learned how to love.

Dear God,
My body hurts, my heart is aching and my mind is a mess.

Please love me.

The incandescent truth
Fills the space between words
That roll off my tongue like rain
Drops down
From clouds of thought
Constructed by strange storms
We make shapes from the pieces
Of evidence we find
To support the point
We've argued the longest.

Those battles are the strongest
The days it takes everything I've got
To find

The incandescent truth
The one that shines between the attacks
Of panic that squeeze my lungs
The air is thin
When I climb too high
Alone on the mountain
I made in my mind
I am breathless

From the weight of all that I store
In a body that needs to dance
I make shapes from my limbs
And nobody is watching.

I have stopped waiting
For somebody to make me numb.

It's only now that I am laid bare
I feel the truth of me

The colours burning bright with their intensity
I only want to share what I have become
Because it is glorious

That incandescence
Shimmers
You have to catch me in the right light
To see it

It's around 10am the morning after
When the glow has not faded
You start to wonder
What you've been in the presence of
And those who do not run

Stay.

I'm not sorry I met you
Now see how I let you
Be the last of lovers
Who didn't know the right way to love me.

I don't know where it will all lead
Only that I trust
I walk in blindness
But feel through my senses
Which way leads to the home I am making space for
In my true heart.

I am preparing for a future filled with love.

It feels as though the earth I'm standing on is solid
That the body I'm in is whole.

Perhaps they always were
And yet
If I hadn't believed that both were broken
I may never have tended to their healing.

I wanted to know if I could capture it
Every moment it took to arrive
Where there is no longer a destination.

It wasn't our first kiss
But it was the one that mattered most
The moment that contained
All I wanted to know.

He liked me.

Of course you knew, he later says
But actually, I had left space
For the possibility of his wanting only to know me
From afar.

A star
Had led me to believe
I might taste the bliss of him again
It wasn't our first kiss
But it marked our beginning.

From the warm water of my mother's womb
To this

A swirling mess of unorganised chaos
Water, blue because sky
You because I
Am I to find solace within
A void where I must sink or swim
Space where silence dissolves in sound
My body knows how not to drown
Instead to ride these rolling waves
Heart open like a cave
The mouth of which will share with me
The bliss of divine ecstasy

Tremors on the ocean floor
Waves crash upon the shore
For a moment I remember water
That I'll always be somebody's daughter
Yet I am woman, reborn
The ocean of my love takes form
As this
Here
Now
You

My infinite sea of blue.

I sought a glimpse
Now I see you *everywhere.*

The sun
The moon
My sacred womb
Rising
Setting
Shedding
Light
Love
Menstrual blood
The cycles of nature
Unending.

He arrives
To find my life in tact
Won't see the cracks in my foundation
Unless I choose to lay them bare.

Perhaps the easier way would be to say
I am delicate and tender-hearted.

Please tread lightly in my world.

Like water you wrap your love around me
Not concerned with the shape we make
But rather the fullness of us
Filling the empty spaces
You know exactly how
And when the tides come in
I'm in love
The bliss of you in the places I have learned to breathe into
And be still

I do not ask you to come
But the moon and stars and celestial bodies orchestrate our symphony from above
You move close
Irresistibly drawn by invisible forces of nature
The laws we long to obey
Attraction, harmonic convergence
We merge in harmony and in love.

Only for a moment
A breath
You yearn for the power you felt as the waves
And I have grown to love the journey
Though you soothe and heal and electrify my senses
We both know we have other parts to play
You return to the sea
I to the wind
Our sacred dance
The song of lovers serenading each other across the play of space and time

Listen to the ocean as he roars
His urge to break, crash, destroy
Wash away

Lick the wounds of Mother Earth
His salty kisses soften and make her sigh

I don't explain our sacred mystery
I become it
Dissolving into bliss
A breath of air
Weightless, restless
I long for distant travel
Foreign lands and desert sands
I rattle at the window, bang on the door
Turn like a tornado
Break hearts in the storm of my awakening

I tell the story of you
Wherever I go.
Water
Fills the cracks we didn't even know were there
In the reflection of your eyes I see myself more clearly still
And when we find the time to rest in one another's arms again
I am quiet
I don't need you to know how I got here
Only that I did
I left and I returned
I love myself enough myself to fall in love with you
To know where you end and I begin
Yet allow us to be one
Allow you the space to look into my eyes and see the truth of your beauty
Unmarried by my story
In which you play the part of water
Wild, infinite and free.

I listen to her speaking
All the truth and wisdom and anguish
Of her ancestors alive in her voice
She has won, by remembering.

You give me the chance to play the part I've always wanted:

Myself.

When

body
mind
heart

align.

We are home
In the heaven we create for ourselves
Through conscious choice.

For the love of God
I show up
With a heart ready to receive
Only then do I have blessings to pour out.

Listen
Without fixing
Be the cup for their emotions
Then pour them
With blessings
Into the earth.

Family
The endless choice we make to love
When our hearts are hurting
To open the door
When we are done with the day
Knowing that where we have been
Has prepared us perfectly
For what is to come.

Thank you for showing me the beauty in your life, he said
Holding me close as we prepared to part
I did my best to hold back tears
But years of heart-opening
Left me exposed.

In prose, I profess to proudly know the way
Out of darkness into the light of day
But having him there,
Knowing as much as he did
And still wanting to stay
Was too much.

I confess, I let those feelings in
The fear of falling and somehow losing
Him, or the part of myself I let him see
When so much of the beauty there
Was created by my love for him.

It was a strange state of being in love and in grief at the same time.
(Author unknown)

I am giving up control
I think I will be surprised by how marvellously
The earth spins on her axis
Without my intervention.

I thank God for you
Every single day.

The poet in me stirs
The artist in me wakes
Across the stretch I look
I keep looking
I can't imagine
There are many places
Left untouched
A single stone
Unturned
Still
I go in search of them
The fragments of my heart
Not yet warmed
By the light of your love.

I stop looking for the answer
Anywhere except my own body.

I am listening
For her footsteps
For now, she is soft
No more than an idea

I will be ready for her when she comes.

Laying in the morning sun
It's the little things in life that truly count
Remembering how breath has the power to bring me life
Lengthen my spine
Lessen the ache in my lungs
Grief clings.
Depths of sorrow
We have to face at times
Suspended between parallel and paradoxical worlds

I am space and chaos
As much star as I am mycelium
The contrast often too striking to consider

Not only is there truth
In being both shadow and light
There is beauty
Profound beauty

Of being all of it in every moment.

Then
When moments arise
That threaten my peace
To steal my spaciousness
I can breathe

Home in the complexity of life
Connected by the simplicity of breath.
My body
A miracle of love.

Lightning Source UK Ltd.
Milton Keynes UK
UKHW040238300422
402201UK00011B/318

9 781649 696793